Cherrie Southerland

JESUS:

DO YOU KNOW HIM?

Volume 1

By

Cherrie Southerland

B.B.M. Publishing

Cincinnati Ohio

Acknowledgements

I would like to thank...

Our Lord and Savor Jesus Christ,

without whom there would be no book.

My daughter **Marla Southerland**,

who helped with the concept of the book.

Lynnette White and **Crystal R. Phillips-Hill**,

who helped with the editing of the first draft.

My **sister Deborah Southerland, Ph.D**.

who was a reader for the draft of the book.

Brooklyn Darkchild,

for her work with the overall editing and formatting of the book and her expertise in the process of self-publishing.

Cherrie Southerland

TABLE OF CONTENTS

Cherrie Southerland

INTRODUCTION

I thought writing this book would be a good way to introduce you to my best friend, *Jesus*. After you read some of the messages I hope Jesus will become your best friend, too. At the very least I hope you'll want to start hanging out with Him.

Think of it like Facebook: After you listen to all the wonderful things that are said about Jesus maybe you'll put in a Friend Request of your own. Or like Twitter, maybe you'll become a Follower. Hopefully you'll start wanting to know more and more about Jesus and begin to understand what the benefits are to being in His presence.

When you get in His presence you'll discover that Jesus will:

Love you when you think you're unlovable,

Have the answers to all your questions,

Make you want to praise Him,

Give you peace that surpasses all understanding,

Show you the way to everlasting life,

Remove shame from your life.

Each chapter in this book is a complete message. I'm so excited about introducing you to my friend. Let's go meet Him. But first, let's start with a word of prayer…

Father God I pray that the Holy Spirit will breathe on the reader of this book and that they will be healed, delivered and set free as they read each message. I pray that they will allow Jesus to become a real friend to them. In Jesus' name Amen.

IT'S A LOVE THING

John 3:16

16 For God so loved the world that He gave His only begotten Son, that whoever believes in Him should not perish but have everlasting life.

John 15:9-17

9 As the Father loved Me, I also have loved you: abide in My love.

10 If you keep my commandments, you will abide in My love, just as I have kept My Father's commandments and abide in His love.

11 These things I have spoken to you, that my joy may remain you, and that your joy may be full.

12 This is my commandment, that you love one another as I have loved you.

13 Greater love has no one than this, than to lay down one's life for his friends.

14 You are My friends if you do whatever I command you.

15 No longer do I call you servants, for a servant does not know what his master is doing, but I have called you friends, for all things that I heard from My Father I have made known to you.

16 You did not choose Me, but I chose you and appointed you that you should go and bear fruit, and that your fruit should remain, that whatever you ask the Father in My name He may give you.

17 These things I command you, that you love one another.

IT'S A LOVE THING

God does not want us just to exist on this earth, we need a purpose. But if we are to have a purpose in this world we need to know God—really know who He is. We know that God shows Himself to us in many ways, but I would like to concentrate on this one: that God is Love. When God created the world, He loved; when He created man, He loved; when He created the animals, He loved; when He selected his chosen people, He loved. When God uncovered His plan to allow the Gentiles to become a part of His kingdom, He loved.

John 3:16 says it best.

"For God so loved the world that He gave His only begotten Son, that who so ever believes in Him shall not perish but have everlasting life."

For God so loved the world. The whole world includes everyone on the Earth. That's a lot of love when you can include every human being on the face of the planet. Some of us can only comprehend loving our family and maybe a couple of friends, some of us not even that many. But what about a God that has so much love that He can take in a whole world...

Well let's think about our families: Everybody in our family isn't loveable, some we don't even like. What about Uncle Ned who drinks all the time and beats his wife and kids, how do you love him? Or Cousin Willie who sells drugs on the corner to little kids? What about Aunt Shirley who sleeps with everybody's husband, or Ms. Maggie who goes to church almost every day, but come home and spends the rest of her time gossiping about everybody?

Where we don't see people as lovable (sometimes including ourselves) God does! He loves them with that special Agape love that is an "in spite of" love. It's unconditional. God loves us in spite of who we are, what we do, what we look like, whether we are rich or poor, Black or White, old or young, sick or well.

He loves us whether we live in the USA, Africa, China, Paris, India or England. His love is for everyone. It's limitless like He is, and He's giving us the opportunity to be with Him forever. And guess what? All we have to do is acknowledge his son "Jesus". Jesus is the only way to the Father.

Who are we to be loved by such as Him? You know we have to learn how to love the person but hate the sin. When my daughter was going through a bad time in her life, she really put me through a lot of pain. I watched her do things I never imagined she even knew about let alone would do, but while *what* she was doing really upset me, I still loved her with a strong, powerful love. A love that would not let me give up on her, but made me continue to fight for her when she wouldn't even fight for herself. If you've been through something like that then you can imagine the kind of love God has for us. It's a love that encompasses far more than we can ever comprehend. God's love includes the murderer, the rapist, the abuser of children, those who take advantage of the helpless—the widows and orphans. And His love is one that we have done nothing to earn. It is simply because of His mercy and grace—a gift if we choose to accept it.

How do we decide to accept it? Well first we need to meet his son Jesus. And just who is Jesus and what can we expect from Him? In the scripture I read, Jesus said, "I loved you as My Father loved Me. Remain in My love. When you obey me, you remain in my love." (John 15:9-10)

Let's meet this Jesus.

Jesus was sent here to be a friend to everyone. And Jesus is a friend like no other. He made the ultimate sacrifice and died on the cross for our sins.

And in return all you have to do is confess with your mouth that Jesus is Lord and believe in your heart that God raised Him from the dead and you will be saved. For it is by believing in your heart that you are made right with God, and it is by confessing with your mouth that you are saved (Romans 10:9-10). When you do that you make Jesus your friend for life. And what a friend!

Jesus cares when nobody else cares. He is there when no one else is there. He loves us when no one else loves us. He stays with us when everyone else has gone. The Bible tells us that Jesus will never leave us nor forsake us, that He will be with us till the end of the ages (Matthew 28:20). By faith we have to know that. We have to know that we will always have a friend in Jesus. Sometimes our best friend is our mother, father, sister or brother, but Jesus will stick closer than any of them.

Like the woman with the issue of blood who spent every penny she had trying to get well, we try everything else before we try Jesus. We have to get into that place where we can hear Him say *"Come unto me, all ye that labor and are heavy laden, and I will give you rest."* (Matthew 11:28) When we are out there snapping our fingers, with the music too loud, we can't hear Jesus. When we are out there working twelve to fourteen hours a day with too much on our minds, we can't hear Jesus. When we are out there feeding our various addictions, we are feeling too good, and we can't hear Jesus. Unfortunately, we have to get to that place where the music has stopped for us, to hear Jesus. We have to get to where we no longer have that job, to hear Jesus. To hear Jesus we have to get to where our addictions have turned on us, and are killing us. But even then, even when we put everything ahead of Jesus, He still loves us and cares for us and is waiting with open arms to help us.

He's that kind of friend.

He was sent here to show us what it means to be a true friend. Jesus, in obedience to His Father, came to seek us out. He wanted to know what it would take to be our friend. He needed to know what it was like to be us. You've heard the saying: "You don't know me until you walk a mile in my shoes." Well He came down and walked a mile in our shoes so He would know what it was like. While He was with us in the world He was tempted, rejected, despised, He didn't even own His own home but depended on the kindness of others, He was hated, loved, He suffered pain and eventually death. He went through it all.

Because it's a Love Thing.

In Luke 8 we find that the woman with the issue of blood was alone. She had been bleeding for twelve years; it was uncontrollable. Can you imagine! No one could touch her or anything she had touched: by law she was considered unclean—so unclean she was to be divorced by her husband. She was totally cut off from society and religious worship. But Jesus never left her.

It was a Love Thing.

The Bible also tells us in John 11 about a friend of Jesus' named Lazarus. On several occasions we see Jesus socializing at Lazarus' home with him and his two sisters Mary and Martha. Well one day while Jesus was out of town word came to Him that Lazarus whom He loved had died. The Bible tells us that Jesus wept: He wept because He loved Lazarus, He wept for His friend. And what did

Jesus do for His friend Lazarus? Well He went to the tomb where they had laid him—his friend who had been dead for four days, and had already started to stink. Jesus gave thanks to His Father for what He was about to do and commanded Lazarus to get up and walk, and Lazarus was raised from the dead. And just as He raised Lazarus from the dead to walk the Earth with Him for a little while longer, He will in the last days raise us up His friends to be with Him throughout eternity. Jesus will do this because He loves us.

He *loves* us.

A friend will love you and have compassion for you. In John 6 we read about a time when a great multitude had followed Jesus to a barren mountain area to hear Him speak and see Him heal the sick. Jesus recognized that the people needed to eat or they would not be able to make the long walk back to their homes. He had compassion for the people, so using the authority and power given to Him by His Father, He fed the 5,000-plus people from two fishes and five loaves of bread. Jesus not only met their needs, they were able to eat until they were full and had twelve baskets of leftovers. Jesus is a friend who will provide for those He loves and those who love Him. John 10:10 says that He came so that we would have life and have it more abundantly.

He's *that* kind of friend.

A friend doesn't belittle you, a friend accepts you as you are. When we think so little of ourselves and isolate ourselves from others—when we see ourselves as not good enough—we can call on Jesus, because He is a friend like no other. In John 4:1-42 The Samaritan woman at the well didn't know she needed a friend until she met Jesus—the Jesus who knew all about her yet didn't make fun of her, who accepted her and offered her living water. Jesus told her she had five husbands and the man she was currently living with was not one of them. But He didn't talk down to her—He accepted the Samaritan woman and offered her a new way of life.

The man at the pool of Bethsaida had been waiting to be healed for thirty-eight years until he looked up and there was Jesus, who had compassion for him and healed him instantly (John 5:1-9). The lepers were just waiting to die until they met Jesus and He healed them (Luke 17:11-14). Just as He did for the woman with the issue of blood, He did for others, and guess what? He will do the same thing for all those who want to be His friend.

Then one day Jesus gave us all the ultimate gift: He died on the cross for us. He who knew no sin died for our sins. John 15:13 says: *"Greater love has no one than this, than to lay down his life for his friends."* Well Jesus made that ultimate sacrifice and died on the cross for our sins, so that we could have the right to everlasting life. He died an awful, painful death and took on all of our dirty filthy sins so that all we would have to do is confess with our mouths that Jesus is Lord, and believe in our hearts that God raised Him from the dead, and we would be saved. He now sits at the right hand of the Father and intercedes on our behalf.

It's a Love Thing.

Now our friend has an adversary, Satan, who doesn't want us to know Jesus as our friend. He doesn't want us to have that personal relationship with Jesus, that intimate relationship that keeps us in constant communication with Him through prayer; that keeps us in His Word every day so we can learn all we can about our friend: so we'll know how to please Him and we'll do what makes Him happy. See Satan doesn't want Jesus happy because it reminds Satan that he is a defeated foe—that Jesus took care of him on the cross.

We need to be aware of the enemy. We need to be

aware of jealous people who try to get between us and our friend Jesus. The ones who say, "You don't have to go to church *every* Sunday. Come on and hang with me today, there's a great One Day Only sale." Because, of course, the sale is on...? Sunday! They tell you, "Oh come on! Let's stop for just one drink before we go to Bible study." Anything to keep you away from Jesus. John 10:10 tells us that: *"Satan has come to steal kill and destroy."* He wants to destroy your friendship with Jesus. We just need to remember that Satan is not a friend of Jesus and he is not our friend, either.

Satan's *job* is to kill, steal and destroy. He will destroy your sense of well-being and have you asking, "Is this all there is? I feel so hopeless. I have everything money can buy, but..." or "I'm at the top of my profession, but...I feel the need to go find myself." Or "I've tried every drug known to mankind, but...I can't find that high anymore. And chasing that first high made me empty my bank account, lose my job, and my family." Many of us will fall into the trap of feeling like no one really loves us or cares about us: right after the love of our lives dumps us, right after we lose a loved one through death, right after we relocate and find ourselves all alone in a unfamiliar setting, right after we lose our best friend, right after everyone has gone and we are alone. That can put us in a place where Satan can attack. We just need to call on Jesus and know that He will never leave us nor forsake us even until the end of the world.

And *that's* a Love Thing.

We are precious in the sight of God: He made us in His image. When God loves us and we love Him, when we have that relationship, there will be no end to that kind of love. It will last through eternity; it will be never ending. And like His Father, Jesus is there when no one else is there.

There was this family who bought a new television set and the neighbors gathered on a Saturday to help them put up the antenna. Since they had only the simplest tools, they weren't making much progress... until a man who was new on the block appeared with an elaborate tool box containing everything they needed to get the antenna up in a hurry. As they stood around congratulating themselves on their good luck, they asked the new neighbor what he made with such fancy tools. He looked at them and smiled and said: "Friends, mostly."

He turned it into a Love Thing.

That's what we need to do with the "fancy tools" we have. We need to use these hands to help someone in need, to give a hug to someone who needs to be touched. We need to use these eyes to read to someone who can't read for themselves. We need to use these ears to listen to someone who just needs to talk. We need to use these feet to run errands for someone unable to do it for themselves. We need to become a friend to someone like Jesus did.

Who have you been that kind of friend to? The first thing we think about is what we *can't* do. I can hear some of you now, saying: "I can't raise anyone from the dead." Can't you? There may be someone you know who is dead to Christ, because they don't know Him; well you need to tell someone about Jesus. Bring them *out of the darkness into the marvelous light*. Tell them that Jesus is *the way the truth and the light and that no man can come to the father except by him*. Tell them that *the wages of sin is death*. Then you need to tell them what He said in Rom 10:9, that: *"If you confess with your mouth Jesus is Lord, and believe in your heart that God raised Him from the dead, you shall be saved."* Yes, you can raise someone from the dead and be a friend like Jesus.

Just as we have a friend in Jesus, someone should have a friend in us. We are told in Matthew 25 to feed the hungry, visit the sick, clothe the naked, and give shelter to the homeless. When we do this we are a friend like Jesus.

Know that it's a Love Thing

We are commanded to love the LORD our God with all our heart, soul and mind first, then to love our neighbors as ourselves. If we can learn to do that, we will do what God wanted for us all along.

To not perish but have everlasting life.

Cherrie Southerland

CHOOSING TO PRAISE GOD
ANY TIME, ANY PLACE, ANYHOW

Habakkuk 3:17

17 Though the fig tree may not blossom,

Nor fruit be on the vines;

Though the labor of the olive may fall,

And the fields yield no food;

Though the flock may be cut off from the fold,

And there be no herd in the stalls—

18 Yet I will rejoice in the Lord.

James 1:2

2 My brethren,

count it all joy when you fall into various trials,

CHOOSING TO PRAISE GOD
ANY TIME, ANY PLACE, ANYHOW

I remember one year I was at an overnight women's retreat, and early in the morning I took my bag to the car before I went to Morning Prayer. When I got back to the building I found that the door was locked and there was no one anywhere to hear me knocking. Did I mention it was freezing cold? After a long while I became very frustrated, especially when I could hear the Morning Prayer and Praise going on inside and I really wanted to be a part of it. Finally, I was no longer frustrated: I was angry! I told God that I was never going to praise Him again because He could have gotten me back inside the building.

He could have helped me.

During a lull in my ranting I heard a quiet voice say: "You will praise Me anyhow." I suddenly stopped my nonsense and started laughing and said: "Yes, Lord, you are right." When the last word left my mouth, the door opened and I went in and joined the morning Praise and Worship service.

Habakkuk also understood how I felt. In the text of

Habakkuk Chapter 3 we hear Habakkuk saying that even though there is no food to eat, even though there are no crops to harvest or no cows to produce milk, even though this could lead to famine, death and desolation,

> 18"*Yet, I will rejoice in the LORD. Yet, I will joy in the God of my salvation.*"

We hear Habakkuk in the midst of all of this choosing to praise God anyhow.

How do we get to where Habakkuk is? You just left the doctor's office where you just got the news of a lump in your breast, and they have scheduled you for a biopsy to see if it's malignant. You start walking down 47th Street and as you walk you see ten and eleven year old boys, some you know, selling drugs on the corner. Then as you continue walking you see your neighbor's daughter working on the other corner. It's 11:00 in the morning and you see men with their bags around their bottles walking aimlessly down the street when they should be at work on somebody's job. You walk past all the doors that use to be stores, but are now just boarded up buildings. You continue walking, wondering why you see so many children out playing when they should be in school. If their parents don't care, then (you allow your frustrations to come in) God, do You?

You see a group of young girls either pregnant or pushing a baby stroller. You turn the corner and you hear gun shots and see people scattering and screaming, and you can't help but cry out in despair, "The police aren't doing anything. God, where are you?"

How do we get to where Habakkuk is in the 18th verse? How do we get to the point where we can choose to praise God any time, any place, and anyhow? I want you to journey with me as we discover how to praise God "in spite of". In spite of sickness, in spite of disease, in spite of depression, in spite of unemployment, in spite of disappointments, in spite of sorrows. How do we get to the place where we can choose to praise God any time, any place and anyhow?

God does not leave us in the dark about anything, that's why He had the Bible written for us. If we look at the text in James 1:2 we learn that becoming a Christian does not mean we won't have any problems. As a matter of fact, it says you *will* have various trials, not *if* you will have various trials. Also in John 16:33 Jesus says: "*In this world you will have tribulations.*" So we know that being saved will not protect us from trials or tribulations.

James also tells us to count it all joy—in some translations it says to consider it all joy. Our attitude about the trials can determine our outcome. We need to make a conscious decision to see God's work in any test or trial we find ourselves in. We, as Christians, need to see ourselves in the Potter's Hands being molded and reshaped and made into a better person. We need to see that God is accomplishing something *in* us and *through* us. Trials test our faith, they increase our endurance, and they can teach us how to depend on God. In the natural we are not happy, we feel the pain of the trial or test, yet using God's eyes, we can rejoice knowing that God is at work in this situation, and we can praise Him for what He is going to accomplish in us. We can rejoice because of what we know.

While we are in the Potter's Hands, He also can take a dull finish and shine us up so we will be able to attract others to our light: to bring others to the knowledge of Jesus Christ. In the book of Acts it tells us about Paul and Silas being beaten and thrown into prison (Acts 16:21-23). They are in pain, locked in chains so they can't move, and I would assume expecting to die. But what did they do? They made a conscious decision to count it all joy and they prayed and sang praises to God. And the other prisoners listened. The text tells us there was a great earthquake that shook open all the doors, and the chains fell off the prisoners. (25-27). The prison guard, assuming they had escaped, was going to kill himself, but Paul stopped him by telling him they were all still there. And because of their actions the guard and his household came to hear the Good News and were saved. (Acts 16:27-32) The power of praise is awesome, and what happened then can happen today. The power of praise can cause your chains of bondage, whatever they may be, to fall off.

Have you ever been on a job where they decided to cut back and everybody starts wondering, "Am I going to be one of the people laid off?" "I can't afford to be laid off: my husband is laid off right now so we *both* can't be laid off!" Well, you should be able to consider it joy and let God use you like he did Paul and Silas. Be a light for those in darkness. When they see you aren't worrying (because you shouldn't be worrying anyway) and they ask you why you are so calm about the possibility of being laid off, you should be able to say: "Well I know a Man who told me not to worry about anything, because He knows all my needs and He will take care of them today and through all my tomorrows. Would you like to meet Him?" When we choose to consider it joy, God will continue to give us reasons to praise Him even through the trials.

To be able to count it all joy and to choose to praise

God anyhow, we need to remember to keep our focus on God, not on our circumstances or trials. If we look at Romans 4:20 it tells us that even though Abraham was childless, and he thought his and Sarah's bodies were beyond child bearing age, he stood on God's promise that he would be the father of many nations. The scripture says he gave God the glory, he gave God the praise anyhow. He kept his focus not on the deadness of their bodies, but on God and who He was. Abraham was able to praise God anyhow. Through faith and praise, at the age of 100 Abraham became the father of Isaac.

We can also look at Jesus and ask the question: What would Jesus do? Let's look at John Chapter 11, where it tells us about Jesus' friend Lazarus, whom He loved. We see Jesus at Lazarus' tomb. The scripture tells us Lazarus had been dead for four days and was stinking, but the circumstances of that situation didn't dictate Jesus' actions. He thanked and praised His Father for raising Lazarus from the dead, and He did this with the stench of Lazarus' dead body coming from the now opened tomb. Then Jesus commanded Lazarus to come forth! And Lazarus came out of the tomb still bound in his grave clothes (John 11: 1-44). Like Jesus we need to praise God regardless of the situation. We also see that He gave God the praise even before the circumstances had changed. See, when we know who God is by faith, we will be able to praise Him. We will know, that we know, that we know, that He will take care of whatever the problem is. Like Jesus we need to focus on who God is and not on the circumstance.

In the book of Daniel, we see where a law was signed that said, for thirty days, if anyone petitioned any god or man except the king, s/he would be cast into the lion's den. Now when Daniel heard about the law he had a choice to make. See, Daniel prayed and praised God three times a day every day since his youth. He could stop praying and praising God and not be punished by man, or continue to pray and praise God and count it all joy. Daniel continued to pray and praise God, and was thrown into the lion's den, but God protected Daniel and no harm came to him (Daniel 6: 1-23). Like Daniel we need to choose to praise God anyhow.

We need to count it all joy and choose to give God the praise, because James 1:12 says: *Blessed is the man who perseveres under trial, because when he has stood the test, he will receive the crown of life that God has promised to those who love him.* When we know that we belong to God our attitude should be: Whatever You say,

Lord, or whatever You do, Lord, it is alright with me. I love You regardless. I love You anyhow and if I love You anyhow I will praise You anyhow. See, You created me from nothing and allowed me to get nourishment and to grow. You made sure I was cared for and that I was kept safe. You made a way for me to receive everlasting life even when I know I didn't deserve it. You made a way for me to breathe the breath of life every day; You didn't have to do that. I did nothing to deserve it. You showed me how to live a life that was pleasing to You and even though I strayed from doing the things I was supposed to do or saying things the way I was supposed to say, You were oh so patient with me and loved me anyhow. Anyhow—when sometimes I couldn't even love myself. Anyhow—when I didn't even want You to see me. You looked at me with such love and compassion and said, "Come back to Me anyhow—I will love you when you can't love yourself." Because we know He loves us with such an unconditional love, we should choose to praise Him any time, any place, and anyhow.

We need to learn to walk in the spirit of joy and not despair, to walk in the spirit of joy and not be discouraged, to walk in the spirit of joy and not be defeated. We need to change the way we think, to turn our attitude about trials and tribulation around. We need to change the negative thinking to positive thinking. We need to know that when we endure with a spirit of joy we get stronger. Nehemiah 8:10 tells us that *the joy of the Lord is our strength*; which confirms that spiritual joy is a powerful source of spiritual strength—that just as Jesus endured the trials of the cross: the beatings, being spit on, being humiliated, He had to consider it all joy in allowing them to nail Him to the cross and dying a painful death.

Jesus had to consider it all joy when, as He was taking His last breaths, He asked His Father to *forgive them, for they know not what they do*. He had to consider it all joy in obedience to His Father. Oh, but the reward...not only the reward of a resurrected life: being seated on the right hand of the Father, with all power in His hands, but of being a Savior for billions of people and being our example of how to consider it all joy. When we stand up against trials and temptation, we become a dynamic witness to all those who see us; we demonstrate the living presence and power of Christ. Knowing this should make us choose to praise God any time, any place and anyhow.

Hebrews 13:15 is clear when it says: "*Therefore by Him let us continually offer the sacrifice of praise to God, that is, the fruit of our lips, giving thanks to His name.*" We need to remove anything that would hinder our praise to God. The basis of our praise is Jesus and His sacrifice. If we keep our focus on Him our praise should not be hindered. He is worthy of our continual praise.

There was a time when Habakkuk found himself going into despair, depression and defeat. He walked through his city of Judah crying out to God about all the violence and corruption he saw all around him. Nothing was being done about it. The wicked outnumbered the good and there was no justice. The world around Judah was at war. Habakkuk wanted to know where God was in all this, and why He allowed it to continue. Habakkuk prayed to God about what he saw, but God just confirmed that yes—it *was* happening, and more was yet to come. That yes—He does care, and in time He will do what is necessary.

Because He is God.

Habakkuk had to make a decision—a choice as to what to do: to stay where he was, in a place of despair, or to move from there and wait on the Lord to change this situation. Habakkuk chose to keep his faith in God, to focus on Him and take his eyes off of the circumstances around him. He had to see the outcome through God's eyes, and through them he was able to praise and worship

God before the circumstances had changed. He was able to say to God: I will praise you any time, any place, and anyhow.

Cast aside all those things that would hinder us from praising God. We shouldn't look to other people to tell us when to praise. Some might say the only time you should praise God is when there is a Praise Team in front of the church, telling you when and how to stand up and praise Him. True praise should take place any time, any place, and anyhow. In that midnight hour when you need help and you need it now, try praising God for all the things He's done for you. Praise will block those fiery darts of lies Satan is sending your way, lies like: "You've got yourself in a situation you can't get out of," so that the Holy Spirit can take over. He will turn all those stumbling blocks Satan has placed in your path into stepping stones.

See, that midnight hour experience is not at the church. It could be in your home, it could be in your car, it could be at the store. You have to be able to call on the Lord and give Him the praise and thanks for taking care of the situation by faith. Any time, any place, and anyhow. You just went to the doctor and she told you that you had heart trouble and it was life threatening. The Word says by His stripes we are healed, Hallelujah! You need to start praising God and send Satan on the run. Remember: he is a defeated foe and has been placed under your feet. You are not looking at what the doctor sees or what he says, your joy is in Christ Jesus; you already know because of Him you have everlasting life. Who can take that away from you? No one can—Jesus died on the cross so you could live forever. Knowing that should bring you joy *and* a reason to praise God.

If we count it all as joy that means *everything*, no matter what. Then we can praise the Lord at all times, in all places and regardless of what we are going through. When we get up in the morning we need to be ready to praise Him. We might get up in our right mind, but without our limbs. We still need to praise Him. We might get up with a roof over our heads in the A.M. but not have the rent money in the P.M. We still need to praise Him. We may leave for work in the morning and have a pink slip in the evening. Yet we need to praise Him. That child who got straight A's through high school just called to tell you she flunked out of college. Yet we will praise Him. That indigestion we had this morning was just diagnosed as the need for a triple bypass this evening, yet we will praise Him. Even though you see giants in your life, even though you see walls you can't climb, even though you see rivers you cannot cross. **Even though**!

You can't see God, either: It's a faith thing that you have to apply to your entire life. No I can't see how those bills are going to get paid, no I can't see how those pains are going to go away, no I can't afford another child—yet there is something deep on the inside of me that I can't explain, and it's just moving up a little higher and a little higher. Like a river flowing within me it's moving up from my belly; I can feel it coming on up to my throat and moving to my mouth and it's at my lips and I can't hold it back, it's just got to come out: **Hallelujah**! Oh God thank You for loving me, thank You for saving me, thank You for never leaving me, oh God! I thank you Lord for just the privilege of one more day.

And I can't stop. I shouldn't have anything else to say because of all the bills and sickness and anger, yet...Lord I thank you for being my bridge over troubled waters, I thank you for a reasonable portion of health and strength, because I can still see, I can still walk. I could lose my house yet—I thank you for being my Jehovah Jireh: my provider—Thank You, yet, I will praise you!

And that's what we have to do. Any time, any place, and anyhow.

When we don't know where our next meal is

coming from, praise Him. When we're sick in the hospital, praise Him When we've received a thirty day eviction notice, praise Him. Why! Ask me Why!

Because He is God!

God—who created the heaven and the earth.

God—the Sovereign One

God—who is my Creator, my Redeemer, my Sustainer

God—for whom there is nothing too hard

God—who will never leave me nor forsake me

God—who said, "Let not your heart be troubled"

God—the Mind Regulator

God—the Heart Fixer

God—the Burden Bearer

God—who so loved the world that He gave His only begotten Son that whosoever believeth in Him shall not perish but have ever lasting life.

People, you should make a conscious decision to worship God, a conscious decision to praise God, a conscious decision to glorify God—any time, any place and any how!

The next time you're at the doctor's office and you're told you have a lump in your breast, before you leave the office I challenge you to say that: "The Word says I shall not die but live and declare works of the Lord!" As you walk down 47th Street I challenge you to do it with a different attitude and with praises coming out of your mouth.

1. When you pass the boarded up stores, say:

"The Word says You shall supply all my needs according to Your riches in Christ Jesus."

2. When you pass the children, hear:

"I have never seen the righteous forsaken nor his seed begging bread."

3. When you hear gunfire, hear instead:

"No weapon formed against you shall prosper."

4. When you pass the drug addicts and alcoholics,

see them through God's eye:

See them delivered and in church praising God.

5. When you pass the pregnant teens and the prostitutes:

see them back in school and graduating from college.

Because nothing is too hard for our God, Praise Him for His mercy and His grace, for His love and compassion.

Choose to Praise God anytime, anyplace, and anyhow.

JESUS IS THE ANSWER

JOHN 14:6

6 Jesus said to him, I am the way, the truth, and the life.

No one comes to the Father except through Me.

JESUS IS THE ANSWER

Once I was asked to speak at this youth service. I hesitated because I was a few years older than some of the participants. I have an eight year old daughter, and when she first said to me something about "Mom, that's the bomb," I started looking for shelter. I thought-there was an actual bomb and it was going to explode (lol). However, I knew that the God we know and serve is the same yesterday (in my day), today (in your day), and forever more (in days to come). Praise God!

All of us today, whether we're young or old, have questions we'd like answers to. Here are some of the questions I think young (and old) may have *now*, or may have asked themselves at one time or another; and a few I hope they have *not*.-

Questions like:

How can God help me?

How can He change my life?

Why would He want to?

What would make Him care about me?

When do I get to meet Him?

When I'm in the projects with bullets flying all around me, where is God?

Can He stop the bullets from hitting me?

When I'm in a prison cell with men waiting to take advantage of me where can I find God? Can He stop them from raping me?

When I wake up at home with my brothers and sisters in a house with no food or heat and my mother is on drugs and I never knew my father, where is God?

Can He put food into our hungry mouths?

When I am miserable and in pain because I don't have anyone to tuck me in at night or to hold me like the families I see on TV, where is God? Can He hold me in His arms?

If God can remove my pain, my hunger, my fear, my sense of nothingness, where is He?

Where is God? Where do I find Him?

Does He live in my neighborhood?

What gang does He belong to?

What color is He?

How will I recognize Him?

Will He know me?

Will He talk to me?

Will He love me?

Will He care for me?

Will He stay with me?

If I get angry, will He run from me?

If I'm dirty and smelly, will He back away from me?

If I'm sick and can't take care of myself, will He leave me?

If I'm old, will I still matter to Him?

If I'm in prison for being a serial killer,

would He want to know me?

I must be a bad person because my parents keep telling me I am. What would He think?

I keep doing things, bad things I guess, because my mother keeps beating me until I bleed. Would God do that?

Who... Is... God?

Tell me who He is, tell me where to find Him, tell me how to make Him love me—me, the unlovable.

Tell me how He can save me from a Hell on Earth that I didn't create.

Did He? Why?

Questions, Questions, Questions...

Well, I am here to tell you that the _answer_ to your questions is _Jesus_!

In John 14:6 Jesus tells us that He is the answer to all human problems:

I am the way, the truth and the life.

Jesus tells us that we need to get to know Him, to develop a relationship with Him. Jesus is the way to the Father because He is the only one who has an intimate knowledge of Him. He is the Truth because He revealed God to us through Himself. He is the life because He is not subject to death: He died to demonstrate His continued life. Jesus was the answer yesterday, He is the answer today and He will be the answer forever more! No matter what the question is, no matter what the problem, Jesus is the answer and the solution.

God is the Father of us all. He created us with love and He created us to love Him back, but we allowed the things of this world to come between Him and us. We did. Man did. When we move away from God, we get weaker and weaker spiritually. This gives Satan the opportunity to step into our lives and tempt us to do things/go places that God would not approve of. We then allow ourselves to get so deep into Satan's activities (sin) that we're unable to get out by ourselves. Satan won't help us because we are right where he wants us to be.

But once we get sick and tired of being sick and tired, we can allow ourselves to call on God to help us. Only then we can remember that, yes—there *was* someone who really cared about us, because He created us with, and in, love. How do we know He loves us? The Bible tells us that *God so loved the world that He gave His only begotten son, that whosoever believeth in Him shall not perish but have everlasting life* (John 3:16). Yes—Jesus is our answer. If you would just take the time to learn about Jesus you would recognize that.

God is our creator, but let's think of Him as our Father, a good father—a father who loves us. And because He loves us He wants the best for us: to protect us and to provide for us. No matter what we do, He will always love us. If God is like our father then we need to think of Jesus as our big brother, who being the oldest is our example of how we should live our lives—how our Father would want us to live. Jesus also will go to the Father on our behalf to ask for what we need. You know how you have that one brother or sister who you knew was the favorite child of one parent or the other? And how you would put him or her up to asking that parent for whatever it was you really wanted because they usually could get it? Well, Jesus can go to the Father for us, interceding, and get what we need.

Remember our scripture—*[Jesus] is the way, the truth, and the life: no man comes to the Father, but by [him].* Jesus is the way, but to get to Him we need to understand some of His truths. Then we can receive life. The Bible tell us that:

[We] all have sinned and fallen short of the glory of God

(Romans 3:23) and that:

The wages of sin is death but the gift of God is eternal life in Christ Jesus our Lord (Romans 6:23)

But to receive that gift we must confess Christ—to believe that He was born, crucified, buried and rose again in three days, and ascended up to heaven and is seated on the right side of the Father (Romans 10: 9-10). If we make this confession, God will provide us with an additional helper: the Holy Spirit, who will help us to understand the Bible (God's teachings), and how we should live our lives.

If we are saved but have allowed sin to come back into our lives, we need to repent. That means to confess our sins, to stop doing them, and to ask Jesus to forgive us. Jesus is quick to forgive us because He loves us.

However, where there is good, there is also evil and that is Satan (the Devil). We need to know him so we can learn to avoid him and his tricks. Satan is God's enemy and he wants to destroy anything good. John 10:10 tell us:

The thief (Satan) does not come except to steal, and to kill, and to destroy, I [Jesus] have come that they may have life, and that they may have it more abundantly.

God has given us all we need to succeed, but Satan's job is to rob us of all that by making us forget we ever had it. He will tempt us with the things of this world—the things that we enjoy the most (lust of the flesh). Things like acceptance, recognition, pride, brand named clothes, money, and sex. He *is* going to tempt us. After all, Satan tried to tempt Jesus, so you know he is coming after you and me.

Satan will whisper: "If you follow Jesus you won't have any friends, you won't have any more fun, and you'll be all alone." This is the same spirit who says: "Do it just one time, you won't get pregnant." Satan sits you down in front of the TV and tells you to watch all the movies with sex in them, all the commercials with sex—and let's not forget the soap operas. He'll have your "bestest" friend whisper in your other ear, "Girl you know he loves you. If I was you I would do it."

We have to remember what Satan looks like. He can look like your boyfriend Tommy, or he can look like your "bestest" friend Sherrie. But where is Satan when you're all alone trying to raise a child, and your friends are going to college and traveling and having new experiences—having fun? And where do you think Tommy is? Tommy has hooked up with your "bestest" friend Sherrie trying to make her number two on his score card. Satan will whisper:-"Just take one hit, you won't get addicted." Yet you'll find yourself up on Church Street or Howard Street chasing the drug of your choice, doing whatever you have to do to get the money. He'll say: "Go get with that group over there. They're having a lot of fun, and nobody tells them what to do or messes with them." Then one day you'll wake up with bars all around you, no longer having fun, and *everybody* is telling you what to do.

You have to know who your enemy is. That person whispering in your ear looks just like any of the sisters and brothers you hang out with or go to school with or date. But Satan is a spirit and a counterfeiter; he'll have you thinking he's your friend. I think we call it peer pressure, and we fall for peer pressure because we want that acceptance and recognition, but it's really just Satan trying to destroy you. He wants to stop you from being what God would have you to be.

Satan will tell you, "I know your mother told you to come home at 8:00, but your friends aren't going home, so it's ok to stay out." or "Your mother told you to clean your room before you go out, but she'll be tired when she come home from work and won't notice." **Warning!** In Ephesians 6:1-3 The Apostle Paul commands us to: *"obey your parents for this is right,'* and to *"'Honor your father and mother,'... 'that it may be well with you and you may live long on the earth.'"*

Money is another tool Satan uses to tempt us. Again, he uses TV to show us all the things-we think we need. Little children will fall out screaming on the floor in a store if they can't have that toy they've seen advertised on TV. Or we just have to have that $300.00 pair of Gym shoes that makes all the basketball players jump higher. Or the latest designer dress. Some of us will get a job if we can, and try to work for it, but even there Satan steps in. He has us work on Sundays so we stop going to church, or stop going to Bible Study because we have homework to do. Beware of his tricks! Others allow greed to cause us to take what we want and end up in jail.

He wants to destroy you!!!

But Satan is limited to what we *allow* him to do, so we have to be aware of his tricks. We must not permit Satan to stop us from doing what is right in the sight of God, and thereby receiving the gift of eternal life.

Now let's look at our answer.

God is omnipresent: He fills the universe and is everywhere at once. If we call on His son Jesus, He is with us in the projects or in the suburbs. He is with us when we're sick or when we're well. He is with us when we think we're alone and no one cares. He is with us when we're young and when we're old. If you leave your hometown on the fastest plane possible and go out of the country, when you get there Jesus is there. Psalm 139 says it best:

"Where can I go from Your Spirit?

Or where can I flee from Your presence?"

Our God is omniscient—He knows all things. He knows us at our worst and He knows us at our best. He knows everything about us. He doesn't see us as we see ourselves, He sees us through spiritual eyes—as our Creator/Father who can love us as we are because He knows our fullest potential: not what we are today but what we can be tomorrow. God's understanding is beyond anything we can comprehend. That's why Proverb 3:5-6 tells us to: *"Trust in the Lord with all your heart and lean not to your own understanding; In all your ways acknowledge Him, and He shall direct your path."* If Satan has you bound you need to turn to the answer, Jesus, because He was sent to set the captives free.

Question: Where will you receive the power to withstand the tricks of Satan? Jesus is the Answer! We learn to ask for things we want at a very early age—I know my daughter did. "Mamma, can I?" were her first words. Well Jesus tells us in Matthew 7:7 to: *"Ask and it will be given, seek and ye shall find, knock and it shall be opened unto you.*" Ask for food if you are hungry, ask for shelter if you need it, ask for help with your school work, ask for help if you are having problems at home.

Ask and Jesus will make a way for you.

In the Bible we see where Jesus fed 5,000+ hungry people, where He healed the sick, where He fought battles for His people; He caused the blind to see and the lame to walk. There is nothing that Jesus won't do for those He loves, and He loves us.

When you accept Jesus as your Lord and Savior **He** will save you from your enemies—His Word tell us that No weapon formed against us shall prosper.

When you accept Jesus as your Lord and Savior **He** will feed you—He will provide all your needs according to His riches and glory in Christ Jesus

When you accept Jesus as Your Lord and Savior **He** will be the mother to the motherless and the father to the fatherless and He will rock you in His bosom.

When you accept Jesus as Your Lord and Savior **He** will never leave you nor forsake you, even until the end of the ages.

If you get angry—

He will give you peace that surpasses all understanding.

If you are dirty and smelly—

He will clean you up whiter than snow.

If you are sick and can't take care of yourself—

He will heal your body.

If you are in prison for the worst of the worst crimes—

He will forgive you and use you to save your brothers or sisters who are in prison with you.

Jesus will wipe all your tears away and tell you how much He loves you—because in 1John it tells us that He is Love.

Your questions can be endless but your answers will always be the same: Jesus is the answer.

Do you want to accept Jesus as the answer to your problems today? Or maybe you did accept Him at one time, but you allowed Satan to blind you to what you knew in your spirit was the truth, and- now you are ready to remove the blinders and step on Satan's head and tell Him that Jesus is your choice and not him? If you are one of these people then you have discovered the answer to all of your questions. If not, I charge you to try Jesus for yourself—to do what the Bible says about Jesus:

"Behold I stand at the door and knock. If anyone hears My voice and opens the door, I will come in to him and dine with him, and he with Me." (Revelations 3:20).

If you answer the door, Jesus will become your answer.

IT'S GONNA RAIN

Genesis Chapters 6-9

7:11 In the six hundredth year of Noah's life, in the second month, the seventeenth day of the month, on that day all the fountains of the great deep were broken up, and the windows of heaven were opened.

12 And the rain was on the earth forty days and forty nights.

Cherrie Southerland

IT'S GONNA RAIN

I think most of us have heard the story of Noah and the ark. It was taught to us in Sunday School and Vacation Bible School. We can remember a large boat being built and the animals going in two by two along with Noah's family. We remember the rains coming and the world being completely destroyed by the racing flood waters. It's good that the story is a familiar one, one that carries a message we need to be reminded of over and over again.

It's the same message that Noah preached time after time to the people who watched him build the ark. See, in Chapter Six of Genesis, God told Noah to build the ark; then in Chapter Seven, He tells Noah that it's time to get onboard. However, between building the ark and entering the ark, there was a period of 120 years. One hundred and twenty years of Noah telling the people that Judgment Day was coming, and that it was gonna rain. That God was not pleased with the way the people were living. That they had made the earth a cesspool of immorality and a society of lawlessness and violence.

Mankind was living to fulfill the desires and lusts of his flesh: living for sexual pleasure, money, possessions,

61

position, power, recognition, and honor. They had forgotten God altogether, living only for themselves. But despite Noah's words, they—like a lot of us—probably just looked up at the sky, saw no clouds, felt no drops of rain, and kept going. And I am sure that as the years went past and the kids grew to adults and saw that same man building that same boat telling that same story, they just laughed and pointed him out as that crazy old man who was expecting a lot of water on dry land.

We need to be reminded today that *it's gonna rain*. Why? Because anyone with "eyes to see" ought to be able to see sin on the increase. As we look around we see things like the need for more prisons—not just for the adults but, for our children: Our children who are out there killing one another over hurt feelings, our children who are getting into gangs because someone is missing at home—a runaway father or a mother who is unable to spend quality time with them.

We need to be reminded when we kill people, not in self-defense, but because we want to know what it feels like, or we need to for a gang initiation, or it makes us feel powerful. We need to be reminded when we need protection from the police officers who are assigned to protect us!

Oh yes, it's gonna rain!

We need to be reminded when we read about famine still existing in our sister countries, the number of homeless people skyrocketing in our own cities, global wars continuing as new leaders come and go. Mass suicides by mislead cults, and terrorist bombings. We need to be reminded when diseases run rampant all over the world because we refuse to control our sexual urges. We need to be reminded when we go to high schools and see day care services being provided and condoms being made available. When sin is accommodated in our schools but prayer isn't, we need to be reminded that it's gonna rain.

We need to be reminded when we see the increase of drug use in this country: in part because now our children are also using illegal substances. They say they get high just to feel good or to remove inhibitions, or in other words: to forget that what they are doing is wrong. Oh yes, we know when something is wrong but, we want to do it anyway—we want to be like our so-called friends who are doing the same thing. We want to be popular, so we pop a pill that lets us forget what we were taught at home, at church, at school, or at Sunday School.

It's happening at all levels of school. Our children don't have to go to some dirty back-alley to get these drugs, they get them in their schools from Billy or Sarah in their Math or English class, or from the kid down the street.

This is a sign of sin on the increase.

We need to be reminded when we see our churches looking like the world. In many of our churches today we find fornication, adultery, drinking, gambling, drugs use, jealousy, backbiting, lying and greed. Yes my sisters and brothers, it's gonna rain.

The world is corrupt, and like Noah and his family we need to come up out of the world. We might meet a new friend at work and think s/he is a good person but, we don't witness to them. Instead, we allow them to draw us back into some of the worldly things we used to do. And then, before we know it, we find ourselves backsliding. We stop going to Bible Study, only show up at church every now and then. Because of sin and disobedience we may easily begin to pay less attention to God's warnings. We stop persevering in our struggle against sin, and slowly drift away from God.

When we get in large crowds of worldly people we are quick to take on their actions. That's why, as believers, we should follow what the Bible says: *Let us not give up meeting together, as some are in the habit of doing, but let us encourage one another all the more as you see the Day approaching* (the day approaching is Christ's return) Hebrews 10:25.

The world would have you believe that it's not going to rain—that it will always be dry and sunny. We get blinded by things we think we want: high paying jobs that end up causing us to lie, steal, cheat, or whatever it takes to get to the top. We get into the world of entertainment where drugs and alcohol and late night parties are the norm. Pretty soon we can't see the clouds in the sky because we sleep all day, we can't hear the thunder over the loud party sounds, and we don't believe it's gonna rain because we missed all the signs.

When violence, sexual immorality, crime, killing, lying, and stealing become the norm, you can't see the storm coming. Judgment will involve the outpouring of God's wrath on the ungodly in a new way—one unequaled in history. God will be forced to destroy the world again, but this time by fire.

2Peter 3:7 says:

By the same word the present heavens and earth are reserved for fire, being kept for the Day of Judgment and destruction of ungodly men.

And then John tells us in Rev 21:1-4:

I saw a new heaven and a new earth, for the first heaven and the first earth had passed away and there was no longer any sea. I saw the Holy City, the new Jerusalem, coming down out of heaven from God. Prepared as a bride beautifully dressed for her husband. And I heard a loud voice from the throne saying, Now the dwelling of God is with men, and He will live with them. They will be His people and God Himself will be with them and be their God. He will wipe every tear from their eyes. There will be no more death or mourning or crying or pain, for the old order of things has passed away...

So yes: It's gonna rain.

Oh! But there is good news. The Good News is this: that just as God provided Noah with an ark to save him, his family and enough animals to repopulate the earth, He has provided an ark for us today. Now this ark, unlike the one Noah had to build, is not made of wood that's 130 cubits by 30 cubits. This ark is so high you can't get over it; it's so wide you can't get around it, it's so low you can't get under it. This ark is from everlasting to everlasting. It doesn't have a certain number of rooms. It will hold a number that no man can number. It is not run by sails or motors or just made to float. It has unlimited power— power to lead you to all truth.

Yes, God is a good God; He came up with a new ark to save those who would believe. And like the old ark, He was very specific about how it was to be prepared. First he looked around to find just the right vessel to carry the savior of His people (the ark) to birth. Then He had to be tried, tempted, and tested to see if He could stand up to all the hardship He would have to go through. He was then filled with love and compassion because He had to care for a multitude of all kinds of people: rich, poor, sick, healthy, old, young, intelligent and illiterate. He was going to allow others to assist Him. So He had to be able to teach those He called out of the corrupt world so they could help carry the Good News message to the people. And just as trees had to be killed and cut down to make the ark of the Old Testament, the New Ark had to be killed, had to sacrifice His life for the people who chose to believe.

Yes, you guessed it: This new ark is Jesus Christ.

Jesus will always open a door for His people. But, what do we do? Do we walk with God and live in holiness? Do we denounce sin? Are we joyously awaiting the second coming of Christ? Or are we still cleaning our houses, not yet ready to receive Him—still entertaining people we would not want Jesus to know were still in our lives? We need to follow the way, the truth and the life, we need to trust in the Lord with all our hearts and lean not to our own understanding, and in all our ways acknowledge him, because if we do that, the Bible says He will direct our paths. Jesus is the way, Jesus is the truth, and Jesus is the life. He is our hope when there appears to be no hope at all.

Oh yes it's gonna rain but, when you have Jesus as your Lord and Savior it's not going fall on you. As Believers, we need to dress for any adverse weather conditions. We should never leave home without our shield of faith or our sword of the spirit (the **B**ible). We should never leave home without them. We need to be prepared for whatever we might come against. When your friends tell you that you need to get high on drugs, alcohol, etc., just tell them "No." You get high on Jesus. When someone tries to get you to join a gang, tell them you're already in a gang—with the Father, the Son and the Holy Ghost. Then ask them if they would like to join your gang. When they tell you that in order to be their friend you have to do what they do, tell them you already have a friend: a friend like none other, one who would never leave you nor forsake you; that you have a friend in Jesus, and ask them if they would like to meet Him. You need to know that you can do all things through Christ who strengthens you. That no weapon formed against you will prosper.

Judgment is coming to all of us; we will be held accountable for what we say and do. We should want to be found like Noah—being about His Father's business. We should be found loving one another, we should be found being a witness for God, we should be found working together in our communities to support the homeless, the orphans, the single parents, the senior citizens...those who are in need. Working toward the day when there will be no homeless shelters, no shelters for battered women and children, no gangs on the streets, no famine, and no wars.

When we come up against trials and tribulation, when the storms of life starts to get us down, we need to think about Noah. Noah kept his focus, and kept his faith in a God who spoke the world into existence in six days. He kept his faith in a God who created every living thing. He kept his faith in a God who supplied all his needs. He kept his faith in a God who was the ruler of all he could see, and all he could not see. So when Man came against Noah and his family—laughing at him, hating him, despising him and probably trying to harm him, Noah just looked to the hills from which cometh his help. He didn't look to the right or the left but, kept his mind stayed on his God. He just kept his hand in God's hand.

Noah had to watch as dry land became a river, then a lake and then an ocean. He had to watch as everything he ever knew—people, houses, livestock, the place where he had raised his family for all those years… he had to watch it all disappear. Noah had to see that a boat which took him 120 years to build was so insignificant on all that water. We can't begin to comprehend the magnitude of something like that.

When we come against situations in our lives that make us want to give up or give in, we need to be like Noah and trust in God; and know that everything is going to be alright. And we can do that if we stay close to Him, walk with Him and talk with Him, and know His Word. When we know that God sent His Son to give us life, and life more abundantly, know that Jesus came to give us peace that surpasses all understanding, know that He will never leave us nor forsake us, know that greater is He who is within us than He who is in the world, know that there is no greater love than the love God has for us, we shouldn't have to be reminded that yes—it's gonna rain. But, when you put your life in the hands of the Man who will cause the rain, you have to know like Noah knew:

That in the end everything is gonna be alright.

SHOW ME THE WAY

JOHN 14:6

6 Jesus said to him, "I am the way, the truth, and the life.

No one comes to the Father except through Me."

Cherrie Southerland

SHOW ME THE WAY

One day while I was helping my sister clean out her office, I noticed this little two page book. I could tell it was old because the pages were starting to turn yellow. The title was:

There's a Hole in My Sidewalk

Autobiography

In

Five Short Chapters[1]

I

I walk down the street.

There is a deep hole in the sidewalk.

I fall in.

I am lost...I am helpless.

It isn't my fault

It takes forever to find a way out.

II

I walk down the same street.

There is a deep hole in the sidewalk.

I pretend I don't see it.

I fall in again.

I can't believe I am in this same place.

But, it isn't my fault.

It still takes a long time to get out.

III

I walk down the same street.

There is a deep hole in the sidewalk.

I see it is there.

I still fall in…it's a habit…but,

My eyes are open.

I know where I am.

I get out immediately

IV

I walk down the same street.

There is a deep hole in the sidewalk.

I walk around it.

V

I walk down another street

Does that sound like a lot of us? We want to change but it's not easy breaking all those old habits, letting go of those people in our lives who just aren't good for us. Well, it's a process and we've got to let go and let God show us the way! Our scripture for this message says it best:

Jesus said to him, "I am the way, the truth and the life: no man comes to the Father, but by me." (John 14:6).

STOP—YIELD—U TURN ALLOWED—DEAD END- ---DANGER-----ONE WAY

These are all familiar signs we see every day. They are put in place to guide us through the streets, control the flow of traffic and prevent us from having accidents. They stop us from having head on collisions with other cars or from hitting people trying to cross the streets. They prevent us from turning the wrong way into oncoming traffic. They prevent us from turning down streets that have no way out. They enable us to miss all the gigantic pot holes that are laying there just waiting to swallow up our unsuspecting cars.

Sometimes you feel like there's a conspiracy between the traffic, the people and the holes in the streets to keep you from making it home safely. Well, just as we read in the story, we too can be walking a course of destruction. Like cars in traffic, we need to pay attention to the signs God has provided to show us the way—the way around all the pot holes that lurk in our paths.

One of the first signs we need to address is the STOP SIGN. When we see this sign it should remind us to stop and ask ourselves: Have I studied God's Word today? Have I STOPPED to see what directions He has for me today? 2Timothy 3:16-17 says:

All scripture is given by inspiration of God, and is profitable for doctrine, for reproof, for correction, for instruction in righteousness. That the man of God may be complete, thoroughly equipped for every good work.

See, as Believers we want to know how God would have us live each and every day. I know for myself that if I get up and don't let anything distract me from going to my prayer room and acknowledging God first, my day goes a lot smoother. The Bible tells us everything we need to know about life because the Word *is* life. John 14:6 says:

I am the way, the truth and the life,

no man comes to the Father but by me.

We need to let him show us the way.

From Genesis to Revelations, God is showing us the

way to an abundant way of living. He is showing us the way to life everlasting. The sad part is that so many of us are not listening to the Word, and because we are not listening to the Word, we are not changing. We are not stopping our old ways. We are just continuing down that same old street when we could be living a more abundant life in Christ Jesus. The Word was given to us to change our lives, but we are not allowing the Word to direct and guide us to a new or different way of living.

The Word shows us the way—

STOP! WRONG WAY! DEAD END! DO NOT ENTER! The Word shows us the way not to go as well, and we will miss the mark every time if we don't pay attention to the signs (The Word). To miss the mark is to sin—to separate ourselves from God. It's to take that turn that says: DEAD END. We should never want to take that road. What we should want is to let God show us a better way.

The Bible shows us the way by telling us the way is Jesus! Jesus is the way, the truth, and the life, and no man will get to the Father but by Him. You can go out and search the highways and byways all you want but: Buddha is not the way, Mohammed is not the way, New Age is not the way! Jehovah's Witness is not the way! **Jesus is the way**! But the way is not a smooth paved street with no pot holes, because as we continue down the street we'll see another sign that says:

ROAD BLOCK! DETOUR! RIGHT LANE ENDS
AHEAD!

As we go through life there will be neon signs flashing on and off trying to catch our attention. When I used to work in San Francisco there was a section of town where there were all kinds of clubs. The men would be outside trying to entice you to come in, describing all the things you could see and do once you went into their club. Gambling casinos will let you drink all you want for free as long as you continue to play. So-called "friends" will tell you to come take a trip with them then introduce you to drugs. Those who claim to have spoken to the dead tell you there is no Heaven or Hell so live life to the fullest, because when you die you just die. These ROAD BLOCKS are being placed by an expert: Satan. He knows just what kind of ROAD BLOCK to set up and where to place it. See, he wants to hinder your progress, he wants to kill you.

Satan's ROAD BLOCKS start in your mind as wrong thoughts. "Well, I know I didn't go to church last Sunday but, this sale is only going to be on one day." Can you see the Sale Sign flashing 60% - 90% off??? It's

Satan's DETOUR sign flashing. "I know I should go to Bible Study but, I worked hard today and now I'm tired." Satan's DETOUR sign. "I'm going to Revival tonight but, before I go, I'll stop by a friend's house." Satan's DETOUR sign. Your friend wasn't going anyway, and they convinced you to stay with them and miss the Revival. And all while this is happening...God is flashing:

STOP! ONE WAY! DEAD END! ON COLLISION COURSE! DO NOT ENTER!

I'll just stop for one drink with the guys

I'll just spend the night one last time

I'll just take one last hit on the pipe

I'll just take one last drag on this cigarette

And let us not forget our good friend Peer Pressure. Peer Pressure will tell you: "Girl, it's ok, everybody does it. You can do it just this one time, you won't get pregnant." And while you are busy nursing your baby, the one who gave you the baby is out with your best friend looking to score again. Or how about this one: "I'm just going to say this about them because it's fresh off the wire. I wasn't there but..." No brakes are being applied, and you're accelerating right through God's signs.

God tried to *tell us* what to do but, we just couldn't get it. So He decided to just scrap that and show us the way. He did this in the form of His son Jesus. God used His son to *show us* the way to live a righteous life, then He paved the way for us to do it—by cleaning the slate for us with Jesus's death on the cross. When Jesus died on the cross He removed those things that would hinder us—that would separate us from His Father: <u>Sin</u>. But God knew even with all that, we still needed something else: Someone who would step in when memory starts to fade. Someone who would step in when eyes get too tired to read the Bible. Someone to step in when we have allowed wrong thoughts to lead to wrong actions: **The Holy Spirit**.

John 16:7-8 says:

Nevertheless I tell you the truth. It is to your advantage that I go away; for if I do not go away, The Helper will not come to you; but if I depart, I will send Him to you. And when He comes, He will convict the world of sin, and of righteousness, and of judgment.

John 16:13 says:

However, when He, The Spirit of Truth, has come, He will guide you into all truth; for He will not speak on His own authority, but whatever He hears He will speak; and He will tell you things to come.

The Holy Spirit is capable of changing any situation. A lot of people stay away from church or Bible

Study because they know it will challenge them to change. And I know I have talked to people who say: "I can quit anytime I want to," or "I'm not ready to come to church yet." These are the ones who drive through God's STOP sign or like some of us, do a Rolling Stop. So this lets us know that we need to listen to the guidance of the Holy Spirit. Jesus left the Holy Spirit with us to help us though Satan's ROADBLOCKS.

Let's look at some of the Holy Spirit's signs.

The Holy Spirit warns us when we are heading in the wrong direction. DEAD END! NOT A THRU STREET—You're giving in to sin. DEAD END! NOT A THRU STREET—You're rebelling against God. DEAD END! NOT A THRU STREET—This road leads to Death.

The Holy Spirit will show us the way by showing us a sign that says: U-TURN ALLOWED. This sign lets us know that no matter what Satan blocks our path with, there is a way out if we choose to take it. That's Repentance— the act of turning from sin and dedicating oneself to change; feeling sorrow, regret, or contrition for having done wrong. We need to take down the barriers against God in our thoughts, emotions, and will. Whatever that barrier is, it can be torn down. Let the Holy Spirit convince and influence you to change. Dare to be different. We need to acknowledge the sin, turn from it, and turn back to living holy.

There's another sign we see the Holy Spirit holding up: YIELD. We need to totally YIELD our lives to Christ, to surrender our whole being to Him. This allows the Holy Spirit to infill us. We are no longer separated from God: Our wrong thoughts turn to right thoughts, cultivate right emotions and take right actions.

Once we have been shown the way in the Word and have corrected our wrong actions with the help of the Holy Spirit, we need to be reminded of one more thing. You know how when you finally make it home safely, after all sorts of obstacles tried to hinder you, you are just so glad that you made it home? Well I praise God: For being a God who had mercy on me, provided traveling mercies, and kept me from all hurt, harm and danger. We need to give God the Praise for what He has done for us and acknowledge who He is through our worship. This will help us stay in right relationship with Him.

God inhabits the praises of His people. If we remember to praise Him, Satan can't come in—the door is slammed in his face every time. We are reminded to praise God in Psalm 150. It tells us that *everyone who has breath should praise the Lord*. We should be active in our praise, to use all of ourselves during our praise. We need to sing, to dance, to lift up and to clap our hands, to kneel, to bow, to put everything that we are into our praise. We should be quick to praise God, even before we receive a blessing— we should praise Him for what He is going to do. Luke 17:11 tells the story of the Ten Lepers, where all ten lepers were healed by Jesus but only one came back to give Him the glory and the praise. The others were healed, but the tenth was also made whole, and received Salvation. God wants our praise and we are blessed twofold when we are obedient.

When we worship God we develop a deeper relationship with Him; to worship Him we have to know who He is, and get in His presence. As we worship Him everything else leaves our thoughts but God. We actively YIELD to Him by lifting Holy hands or kneeling. In the book of Joshua chapter 6 we see Joshua and the Israelites being obedient. God told Joshua to have the priests march around the wall surrounding Jericho seven times blowing trumpets before the Ark of the Covenant (which is a form of worship). The people shouted (like our praise) when Joshua gave them the signal, and the walls of a city fell down. If praise and worship can knock down the walls of a city, what can it do to the walls you walk around carrying?

Can it knock down your wall of poverty, your wall of cancer, your wall of diabetes, your wall of loneliness, your wall of family problems, or your wall of secret sins? Of course it can! God shows us the way through praise and worship.

All the signs point to Jesus as the way, the truth, and the life. When you start asking questions like: "Is this all there is to this life?" or "Why should I get up in the morning? I'm tired, and I'm sick and tired of being sick and tired. I feel like I have no reason to live," then **you need a life changing experience**! You need to get in the presence of Jesus. When we get in His presence things are going to change.

Saul met Jesus on the road to Damascus and he went from persecuting the Christians to preaching the Gospel and writing thirteen books of the New Testament (Acts 9). Zacchaeus, a tax collector, met Jesus on the road, and Jesus knew his name. Oh, he knows our name and everything about us. Zacchaeus, a very rich person, served Jesus dinner at his home, and Zacchaeus and his entire household were saved. Zacchaeus also pledged half his wealth to the poor, and said if he overcharged anyone on their taxes he would give them back four times as much (Luke 19:1-10). If you get in the presence of Jesus (at church or Bible Study), you will hear people give their testimonies of how Jesus visited them in that midnight hour and how their lives were drastically changed.

Rev 3:20 says:

Behold I stand at the door and knock. If anyone hears My voice and opens the door, I will come in and eat with him and he with Me.

Jesus wants us to get in His presence so that our lives will be changed.

Where are your pot holes today? Again we see it is a process to get out of the ruts that life tricks us into, the holes we keep falling into over and over again, but that process begins and ends with Jesus Christ. You don't have a problem God can't solve. There is no hole too deep for Him to get you out of. **He is the way**—but we have to follow Him. **He is the way**—but we have to listen to Him. **He is the way**—but we have to obey Him. If you let Jesus show you the way, you will be set free. I guarantee it. So, my Brothers and Sisters, you need to hear Him tell you to STOP! YIELD! U-TURN ALLOWED! Then get on the street that will take you straight to Jesus.

FOOTNOTE:

    [1] "Autobiography in Five Short Chapters" from the

book *There's a Hole in My Sidewalk: The Romance of Self-Discovery* by Portia Nelson (P)1977 Popular Library, reissued in 1993 Beyond Words Publishing

WHEN THE MASQUERADE IS OVER

Genesis 2:25

25 And they were both naked, the man and his wife,

and were not ashamed.

WHEN THE MASQUERADE IS OVER

We should be able to stand before the Lord unashamed in our spiritual nakedness. In our physical nakedness most of us would not want to. We all have things we don't want anyone to see. We wear special clothes to hide the fact that we are too "something":
Too large. Too tall. Too short. Too small.

Oh, we *will* find ways to hide what we don't want seen.

How many of us were told that black clothes made us look slimmer? That long tops hid big hips and behinds? We wear girdles to pull in big stomachs or long line bras to help the midriff bulge. I have a friend who would never let anyone see her without makeup. We also see men wearing jackets in the summer and sweating, just to hide bulging stomachs, or wearing suspenders instead of belts to allow for increase growth around their waists.

A lot of us are ashamed of how we look. Skinny people want to gain weight; heavy people want to lose weight. We spend major money changing our hair, fixing our nails. I've never seen such a sudden explosion of beauty supply stores and nail salons, and we do it because we care about how other people see us. I remember that if my mother went to the grocery store (back when you walked to the store) she was color coordinated and had every hair in place. That was how she wanted people to see her. There was also a time when you just saw people wear sunglasses outside; now they wear them inside, and they wear them so dark you can't even see their eyes.

Yes, we care what people think about the way we look.

With some of us, our mask is not hiding extra pounds or grey hair, it's hiding pain. Pain that comes from guilt, fear, unforgiveness, rejection, or not liking oneself. Not wanting to admit that sometimes these are the causes of our pain, instead we choose to blame everyone else.

We don't want anyone to know so, we wear a mask.

When the man and woman stood before God naked and unashamed, they were perfect beings, completely innocent. They had done nothing wrong. They had no guilt, no worries, no failures, no fears, didn't know pain or suffering, and most of all: there was no sin. There was no reason to hide behind a mask of any kind. But once sin was introduced we were unable to stand before God naked and unashamed (as if we could). We started hiding behind masks.

There are different reasons why we hide behind a mask. Some people wear a mask of fear: fear of the unknown, fear of not being good enough, fear of what other people will say, fear of failure, fear of not being liked, or fear of loneliness. But the Bible says:

God did not give us the spirit of fear, but of power, and of love, and of a sound mind (2 Timothy 1:7).

We need to take off that mask.

Some put on a mask to hide depression, but the Bible says to: *"Be anxious for nothing"* (Philippians 4:6).

We need to take off that mask.

Some wear a mask to hide poverty or lack. They are afraid to let people know they're in need. They'll go to great lengths to have other people think they have a lot of money—go into debt, write bad checks, even steal to cover it up. But the Bible says:

God will provide all your needs according to His riches and glory in Christ Jesus (Philippines 4:19).

We need to take off the mask.

Some people wear a mask to cover up shame—shame that they are an abused spouse, shame that their spouse is cheating on them, shame that the one they are with is not theirs to *be* with, shame that they have allowed a life of addiction to lower their standard of living.

But the Bible says:

Come to me all who are heavy laden and I will give you rest (Matthew 11:28). It says to:

Cast your cares upon Him, for he cares for you (1Peter5:7). It says that:

No weapon formed against you shall prosper (Isaiah 54:17). It says:

He who is in you is greater than he who is in the world (1John). It says that:

We are more than conquerors through Him who loves us (Romans 8:37).

We need to take off the masks.

We will wear a mask because we're sick but we don't want anyone to know how sick we are. The Bible says: *By His stripes you are healed* (Isaiah 53:5)

We need to take off the mask.

We also wear different size masks. We can see the need for a full mask that covers our whole face when we're hiding sins like murder, armed robbery, sexual sins, adultery, or addictions. But what about those "little" sins? If we only wear the type of mask that just covers the eyes and a little part of the nose, we think that's okay, right? Because these types of masks just hide the "minor" sins of lying, gossip, jealousy, envy, strife, backbiting, mumble-

and-grumbling and hatred. Yet the Bible tells us that even with these "minor" sins, *those who practice such things will not inherit the kingdom of God* (Galatians 5:21).

If we look in Acts 5, we see that Ananias and his wife Sapphira sold a possession and were supposed to give the proceeds to the church. But Ananias lied about how much he received from the sale of the property then told his wife to lie also. He and his wife were killed for trying to deceive the Holy Spirit.

We need to remove those masks.

Some of us Mask Wearers think if we stay busy and keep moving—join three or four ministry groups, attend all the worship services and shout the loudest—our masks won't be noticed. Take a look at our churches today: you'll find groups of half-saved, half-sanctified, carnal people who don't know the Word of God but can tell you word for word the story lines of their favorite soap operas or reality TV shows.

It's time to take off the masks.

No matter what the situation, God can handle it. The Bible says that:

Nothing is too hard for God (Genesis 18:14).

We just need to know God for ourselves. To do this we need to get in His Word--to find out who He is and how He wants us to live our lives. We have to come before Him naked, and let Him see us as we are. We need to show ourselves to God unashamed in our dirt, unashamed in our filth, unashamed in our fears, unashamed in our sickness, unashamed in our feeling of worthlessness.

We need to show it all to Him and allow Him to meet us where we are and begin to clean us up. To gently wash away every bit of sin we've been carrying around: sin that is weighing us down, keeping us chained up— bound up. Because that's what Satan does: he keeps us in bondage by having us think we're too dirty for anyone to stand the sight of us without our masks on. So we walk around with that weight of shame bowing us lower and lower, keeping our heads down so we never look up and see Jesus looking at us. Not with a look of disgust, but with a look of pure love and compassion, ready to pull us out of the miry clay, ready to wash us off and set our feet on solid ground. We just need to take off the mask and stand before God unashamed of how we look.

Once we know how much He loves us—that He will forgive us seventy time seven—His Love will transform us into a new creation. The old things will pass away and all things will become new. We can step into the newness of life and walk tall; be that caterpillar that changes into a butterfly.

Instead we allow Satan to keep us covered up and in hiding. We believe what he tells us, we fall for his tricks. Why do we allow this to happen? Why? Because we won't take the time to develop our own personal relationship with God: to spend time with Him and to really get to know Him. We may know what other people say about Him, but what do we know for ourselves? He has given us, by His unmerited favor, twenty-four hours a day. Can't we set aside one or two of those hours to get to know the one who gave us life?

Jesus suffered and died on the cross for us, so we wouldn't have to wear a mask. Can't you do something for Him? He continues to woo you, to court you, to offer you life everlasting. When the masquerade is over, where do you want to be? I know where I want to be: I want to be standing before God naked and unashamed.

The Word says to seek God, to ask for what you want. It says you can have what you ask for. Satan will keep you silent; keep you thinking: *He can't hear someone like me. I'm too bad; what I have done is unforgivable.* Satan wants you to believe that. It's why he keeps you away from the Word: He needs to keep you ignorant, so he can destroy you, kill you. You need to understand that Satan wants you dead, and he knows the Word of God is life!

Jesus knows what that's like. The Bible tells us Jesus was despised and spit on; beaten. Jesus walked among the poor, the destitute, prostitutes, the sick, and the possessed. He understands our problems. That's why He was sent. He was sent to deliver us from the burdens life has placed on us. To heal us from the pains and affliction life has dumped on us. To provide comfort from all the weights life has laid on us. Jesus said: *Take My yoke upon you… for My yoke is easy and My burden is light* (Matthew 11: 29-30). If we accept His burden, He will accept ours. We need to take His yoke and say, "Yes, I believe in You and I believe in the Father. Yes, I know I have sinned against the Father and I'm sorry. Forgive me." Then give Him all our burdens, our cares and concerns; give Him our sickness, our shame, our insecurities, our addictions—He can handle our heaviest burden. We simply need to decide to give it to Him.

We need to agree to take His yoke of new life: a new life of joy unspeakable, a new life of peace that surpasses all understanding, an everlasting life. A new life of praising and worshiping a God who keeps love in our lives because He *is* love. He will keep us in perfect peace because He is the Prince of Peace. He will give us wisdom because He is that Wonderful Counselor. He will never leave us nor forsake us because He is the Everlasting Father. He will free up our minds from trouble because He is that Bridge over Troubled Water. He's that Hedge of Protection from our enemies, He will take you to that secret place. You won't walk a crooked path because He will order your steps and direct your path.

Don't try to fix your life with a bandage when you can have Jesus:

Jesus - the Heart Fixer and the Mind Regulator

Jesus - the Bright and Shining Star

Jesus - even Xerox can't copy

Jesus - Domino's can't beat His delivery

Jesus-who Michael Jordan or LeBron James can't outscore

Jesus - can make you feel better than your mother

Jesus - He can take you higher than crack

Jesus - can last longer than the Energizer bunny

Jesus - can beat unlimited talk and text, because He's free.

Jesus- better than the Metro because He doesn't make you wait—He says: *Knock and the door will be opened unto you.* (Matthew 7:7, Luke 11:9)

To remove the mask, we need to get to know the Jesus who the woman at the well met: the Samarian woman who was hiding behind the mask of living with a man who was not her husband. She allowed Jesus to remove her mask and send her out to tell the people about Jesus and His living water (John 4: 7-29).

To remove the mask, we need to get to know the Jesus who the woman brought to Jesus by the Pharisees wearing the mask of adultery met. Jesus did not judge her, but told her to: *Go and sin no more* (John 8:11). She was able to leave without her mask knowing her sins were forgiven.

To remove the mask, we need to get to know the Jesus who the Paralytic man lowered through the roof met. Because of his faith Jesus forgave his sins and he was healed. Jesus removed his mask of illness, of not being whole.

To remove the mask, we need to get to know the Jesus who the woman with the issue of blood met. She crawled on her hands and knees through the huge crowd of people, telling herself as she inched her way toward Jesus with each shove and pull that: "If I can just touch the hem of His garment I will be made whole (Mark 5:28); I will become clean again. I can stand upright and walk with the people again: no longer bowed over with shame, no longer shunned and ignored, no longer too weak to do the things other women take for granted." She was healed and her mask was removed.

To remove the mask, we need to get to know the Jesus who the leper met. He fell before Jesus on his face and said, *"Lord if you are willing you can heal me and make me clean." "I am willing," He said. "Be cleansed." And immediately the leprosy left him.* (Matthew 8:2-3, Mark 1:40-41)

The leper's mask of shame at being unclean also fell off of him. He was no longer cut off from him family and friends, from his home and church; he no longer had to just barely exist until his impending death. He was free from the slavery of his illness.

His mask fell off.

These people were wearing masks: masks of pain, shame, uncleanness, sexual sin, illness… but then they met Jesus, who just asked them to:
Believe in me and …your yoke will be easy and your burden light (Matthew 11:30).

None of us who are wearing masks wants to be exposed, but God knows we will *have* to be, so He will send the Holy Spirit to do the job. He had to expose Peter's

Mask of Weakness, when Jesus told Peter he would deny Him three times. Like Peter, we'll deny over and over again that we are wearing a mask. What we really need to do is repent, to ask God to forgive us for our failures and wrong doings, and to totally lean and depend on Him. If we would just do that, the masks would start falling off.

We need to be reminded that God is our Creator, and since He is All Knowing, He already knows all about us. God knows our troubles, our weaknesses, our sins... and guess what?! He loves us in spite of it all!

God wants us to be able to stand before Him naked and unashamed, and we can only do that if we allow Him to help us. We need to yield to Him, put our complete faith and trust in Him, and stop trying to do it ourselves. Once the masks come off look what can happen:

Abram became Abraham—father of many nations;
Jacob became Israel—Father of the chosen people;
Rehab—a prostitute—became the great grandmother of King David;
Saul of Tarsus became The Apostle Paul—who preached the Good News to the Gentiles, and wrote most of the New Testament.
And I became a preacher of the Gospel.

Remove your mask and let God's plan and purpose for your life be fulfilled.

It's Time.

It's Time.

It's Time, people.

It's time to take the masks off… the masquerade is over.

Cherrie Southerland

BIOGRAPHY

Cherrie Southerland is an ordained minister currently on the ministerial staff at the House of Joy Christian Ministries in Cincinnati Ohio. While living in Chicago IL in 1994 Ms. Southerland entered into the ministry. She loves the Word of God and enjoys preaching and teaching the Word of God in the various churches she has been associated with. Most of all, Ms. Southerland enjoys telling a story, and finds this is a good way to get God's message to the people. She is a retiree, the mother of one and grandmother of one.

Ms. Southerland's favorite scripture is: "But seek first the kingdom of God and His righteousness, and all these things shall be added to you". (Matthews 6:33)

You may contact her at mincls47@gmail.com

Look for Volumes 2 and 3 coming soon from BBM Publishing!

Cherrie Southerland

www.ingramcontent.com/pod-product-compliance
Lightning Source LLC
Chambersburg PA
CBHW060951040426
42445CB00011B/1101